P9-EFH-074

BLAIRSVILLE SENIOR HIGH SCHOOL
BLAIRSVILLE, PENNA.

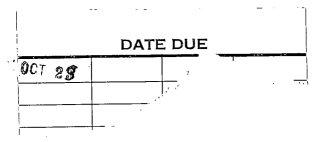

DATE DUE

OCT 2 9				

OMAR KHAYYÁM, the Persian astronomer-poet, was born at Naishápúr, in Khorastan, in the eleventh century A.D., as Abu'l-fat'h 'Omar, the son of Ibrahim the Tentmaker. He took the word for his father's trade, Khayyám, as his poetic name. Omar spent his entire life in his native town, but became known far and wide as a scholar and astronomer, and was the author of astronomical tables and a book on algebra, as well as the Rubáiyát. He died in 1123.

"Omar was a man of subtle, strong, and cultivated intellect, fine imagination, and a heart passionate for truth and justice; he flung his own genius and learning with a bitter or humorous jest into the general ruin. The result is saddest perhaps when most ostentatiously merry: more apt to move sorrow than anger."

Edward FitzGerald

THE RUBÁIYÁT OF OMAR KHAYYÁM

Complete English Translation
by
Edward FitzGerald

with biographical notes,
critical commentary, and
aids to appreciation
by Dr. Marcus Konick

An Avon Library Book

AVON BOOKS
A division of
The Hearst Corporation
959 Eighth Avenue
New York, New York 10019

First Printing, July, 1941
Twelfth Printing (Avon Library), October, 1967
Thirteenth Printing, February, 1969

Cover illustration by Robert Pepper

Printed in the U.S.A.

Contents

FOREWORD

It is rare indeed when critics and the lay public agree that a work of literature is among the great achievements in our language. Yet such is the opinion held of a work which is in origin a translation from a far-off language and time. It is a poem which is sensuous, but perceptively analytical; melancholy, but urging that mankind take advantage of those delights which have been granted by a careless but omniscient Force. The poem is the *Rubáiyát* of Omar Khayyám, little known to any but a handful of scholars until re-created in a foreign tongue, climate, and culture seven and a half centuries later by Edward FitzGerald.

So compelling is the melody of this poem that it is easy to forget the sensitive minds behind it, bemused by the conundrum of existence, yet with the courage to resist both platitudes and the charge of heresy. In the hope that the song of the poets who created it might be the better appreciated and the implications of its thought better understood, we publish again the *Rubáiyát*, illuminated by notes, commentary, and questions for discussion. Thus its significance for contemporary man can, we believe, be enhanced.

Tennyson paid the translator of the poem and his lifelong friend the ultimate tribute with which the world has ever since with rare unanimity agreed: –

> Who reads your golden Eastern lay,
> Than which I know no version done
>   In English more divinely well;
> A planet equal to the sun
>   Which cast it, that large infidel
> Your Omar; and your Omar drew
>   Full-handed plaudits from our best
>   In modern letters. . . .[1]

1. Tennyson, Alfred Lord, "To E. FitzGerald," *Tiresias and Other Poems.* London, Macmillan and Co., 1885.

LIFE OF OMAR KHAYYÁM

Ghiyas Uddin Abul Fath Omar Ibn Ibrahim al-Khayyámi was not only a poet but an astronomer and mathematician. He was born in the middle of the eleventh century in Nishápúr, Persia, but was probably descended from Arabs who, fleeing from religious or political violence, had taken refuge in Khurasan. He himself stated that he lived to be over a hundred years old, although what evidence we have indicates that he may have been born about 1044 A.D. and died in 1123 or 1124.

FitzGerald believed a story told by Nizám al-Mulk in the *Wasiyat* (Testament) to the effect that Omar was one of three pupils of the Imám Mowaffak of Nishápúr, who pledged that they would share whatever prosperity they achieved. Nizám became administrator of affairs as vizier to Sultan Alp Arslán and Malik Sháh. Accordingly, his schoolmate Hasan ibn al-Sabbáh came to claim a place in the government as his share of his friend's good fortune. This was granted, but he was discontented at his slow advancement and became the leader of a band of fanatical outlaws who were reputed to take hashish, thus giving rise to the name "assassins." They terrorized both Christians

9

and Mohammedans, and ultimately killed Hasan's former friend, Nizám. However, Omar is said to have requested only peace and a pension, which were awarded him. He rose in favor as an astronomer, mathematician, and wise man.

However, modern scholars believe this story is spurious, for the *Wasiyat* has been proved to be of fifteenth-century origin and there is reason to believe that the Hasan of the story was confused with a later prime minister.

What is certain is that Omar and his father were tentmakers, as their names indicate. The poet himself was an *imam* or priest, who became famous for his wisdom. He had a remarkable knowledge of Arabic philosophy and the Koran. So great was his reputation as an astronomer and mathematician that Malik Sháh appointed him one of eight astronomers to reform a calendar which was inaugurated on March 15, 1079. Gibbon says that it surpassed the accuracy of the Julian calendar and approached that of the Gregorian. Omar wrote one book on algebra and one on geometry, as well as other works concerning mathematics, meteorology, and metaphysics. Having studied the works of Avicenna, the great Arab physician and philosopher, he also wrote on medicine.

Omar's verses are now well known to both the Western and Eastern world because of FitzGerald's translation, though the Persian's heresy had resulted in their being almost unknown in his own country. Discoveries of earlier manuscripts than those used by the English poet (the earliest Bodleian Ouseley manuscript is dated 1460-6), together with the attribution of stanzas to other writers, resulted

10

at one time in a scholarly hypothesis that Omar was the actual author of only thirteen "quatrains." However, in 1949 Mr. Chester Beatty published a manuscript by Mohammed al-Quawám of Nishá-púr. This was reliably dated 1259-1260. In the same year, a Teheran manuscript appeared, transcribed by Ghiyáth al-Din Mohammed ibn Yúsúf ibn 'Ali in 1207, only 75 years after Omar's death—too soon for any legend to have developed. The former manuscript consists of 172 stanzas, the latter of 252. They firmly establish Omar's right to be considered a significant poet.

It has been suggested that the *Rubáiyát* is a religious allegory. This is based on the assumption that Omar was a Súfi, as were many of the best Persian poets of the period. The Súfis were pantheists who believed that the individual soul, once part of God, could find salvation only in being reabsorbed in Him again, after renunciation of all earthly desires and pleasures. Because the Mohammedans considered them heretics, they had to express their doctrines symbolically. However, Omar ridiculed these religious mystics (see Stanza LV, First Version) and antagonized them. Yet, since he believed in acquiescing to conditions as he saw them and had little faith in the pleasures of the afterlife, the Mohammedans also regarded him as a heretic, and his works were little read in Persia for centuries. Neither Cowell, the Sanskrit scholar, nor FitzGerald, who was his student, considered the poet a Súfi, and modern scholarship has tended to support this view.

It is generally agreed that the verses are the work of an honest and learned scholar who detested

11

LIFE OF EDWARD FITZGERALD

(1809-1883)

The author of what has been called one of the
five best translations in the entire galaxy of English
literature [2] was a shy, irresponsible, eccentric fellow—yet witty and warmhearted. Although his
most famous work praised indulgence in pleasures
and his family was one of the wealthiest in England, he lived an abstemious life devoted to "plain
living and high thinking." His chief indulgences
were reading, scholarship, boating, smoking, and
a host of lifelong friends.

Edward FitzGerald was born Edward Purcell
at the White House, Bredfield, Suffolk, England.
He was the seventh of eight children born to
John Purcell and Mary Frances (née FitzGerald),
both descended from companions of William the
Conquerer. When Mr. FitzGerald died in 1818
and left his daughter the family fortune, the Purcell family adopted his surname.

2. Walker, Hugh, *The Literature of the Victorian Era.*
London, Cambridge University Press, 1921, pp. 482-3. The
other four are the authorized version of the Bible, Chap-
man's *Homer,* Pope's *Homer,* and Jewett's *Plato.*

Edward's lifelong lack of ambition can be traced to the stern discipline of his home, with a father who preferred the life of a country squire and a mother "handsome, clever, and eccentric" who ignored her children while she sought a fashionable and cultured life in London. The boy therefore learned early to love both the open countryside and the seacoast (where the family spent many a summer), and the theaters, concert halls, and art galleries of London and Paris.

The family had little respect for the "scribbling of verse," and Edward turned for his interest in literature to a friend and neighbor, Major Edward Moor, a retired officer in the Indian army, who had published *Oriental Fragments* and a dictionary of Suffolk provincialisms.

Edward was not an ambitious scholar, whether at the small private school at Woodbridge, near his home, at King Edward VI's Grammar School at Bury St. Edmunds, or at Trinity College, Cambridge. At the university, he took the least demanding course, and withheld himself from the company of a group of intellectuals called the Apostles, of which Alfred Tennyson was the leader. However, he knew most of them personally. Yet he loved Cambridge and returned to it often in later years. There he developed lifelong friendships with William Bodham Donne, who was descended from the poets Donne and Cowper and became a celebrated librarian; James Spedding, who edited the works of Francis Bacon; John Mitchell Kemble of the acting family; William Makepeace Thackeray; Alfred Tennyson and his brother Frederick. He soon came to know also Thomas Carlyle, Charles

Lamb, the Crabbes, Samuel Laurence, William Wordsworth, Charles Dickens, Swinburne, the Brownings, the Rossettis, Ruskin, and other writers and artists. He maintained a voluminous correspondence with his friends and this has since been declared his second claim to fame, for he became one of the celebrated letter-writers of his century—relaxed, witty, penetrating, earthy, giving his observations on life and literature in a fashion perhaps biased but always intriguing. Moreover, his friendships were said to be more like loves, for he would spare no pains for a friend, whether to lend him money (unobtrusively to avoid offense), find him commissions, or offer the hospitality of his house while he confined himself usually to a single, cluttered room.

Although Edward's father lost his fortune in coal-mining and the poet himself suffered reverses, he always had enough to maintain himself in comfort and without concern, always enough to help a friend, and unfortunately perhaps always enough to prevent his having to work with the assidity which produced the works of men he admired like Scott, Thackeray, Dickens, and Carlyle.

After his graduation from the university, Edward spent some time escorting his mother and sisters on their visits to the theater, art galleries, and homes of friends and relatives. He did not mind very much, for he was very fond of both art and children. As to his personal social life, he always visited friends, and they him. His first love had been Elizabeth Charlesworth. However, while he delayed his proposal, she had married Edward Byler Cowell, then a merchant, whom she so encouraged in his studies

15

that he ultimately became professor of Sanskrit at Cambridge. After this disappointment—and it seems to have been deep—Edward found himself involved in an obligation forced upon him by his friend Bernard Barton, the Quaker poet, who at his death had joined Edward's hand with that of his daughter. After a seven-year engagement, and with no hopes of happiness, Edward, then 47, married her. She was one year older, intelligent, ambitious, large-boned, and loud-voiced. What was worse, she had social pretensions and he detested ostentation. They had a large wedding, for which he appeared in his old clothes and a slouch hat. Within four months they were separated. Edward returned to his celibate life with guilty delight.

FitzGerald preferred traveling about as he wished, boating on the River Deben and off the coast in the *Scandal*, smoking in his old jacket, sketching, playing the piano, collecting paintings, and studying. His ardent friendships continued, most notably with a young herring fisherman, "Posh" (Joseph Fletcher), whom he sought to set up in business but who resented the advice of his patron. Fitz-Gerald's greatest delight was an evening over his pipe, drinking and talking with his cronies.

Without question the friend who meant the most to his development was Edward Cowell, who continually stimulated both his learning and his writing. FitzGerald had learned Latin, Greek, and French at school. Under Cowell's tutelage he studied Spanish and Persian, and then taught himself Italian and German. He preferred to read great works in the original, making notations, and often editing, condensing, synopsizing, and revising them.

FitzGerald published relatively little, sold almost nothing, usually printed his work at his own expense and almost always anonymously. He was constantly busy writing. His first published literary effort was a poem, "The Meadows in Spring," in 1831. His happy life at Cambridge ultimately inspired *Euphranor* (1851), a Platonic dialogue in which he attacked the English educational system and urged that more attention be paid to physical education and practical training for life. The passages he had culled from his reading, in addition to his own aphorisms and comments, he published as *Polonius: A Collection of Wise Saws and Modern Instances* (1852). These are briefs quotations on 139 topics such as Honesty, the Poor, War, and Vanity, from authors such as Carlyle, Bacon, and the classical writers. Largely from his friend Posh he gathered the provincialisms of the Suffolk coast and, when he had quite a collection, discovered that others were doing the same, and sent them his. He had assisted Barton's daughter in editing her father's verse and wrote a memoir to precede it. He had always admired Crabbe's humor and, partly encouraged by his friendship with the family, edited his *Tales of the Hall*, and published it as *Readings in Crabbe* (1879, 1882, 1883). At his death he left unfinished his biography of Charles Lamb and his *Dictionary of Madame de Sévigné*, which was edited by his niece Mary Kerrich.

But probably his most significant work was his translations. He believed that the ideal translator must be transfused with the same spirit as activated the original, yet must adapt the work to the language and philosophy of his own people. Accordingly, his translations were free and, since he always honestly indicated in his prefaces that he had edited and adapted the original, he often was accused of being unscholarly by the reviewers and given short shrift. His study of Spanish (begun only in 1850) resulted in *Six Dramas of Calderon* in 1853. He modestly confined himself to less celebrated works since he wished to reduce the bombast, the artificial phraseology, complexity of plot, and repetitions. He later translated two more plays, which were not published until 1889, when his collected works appeared.

He had begun translations of Greek drama in 1857. In 1869 he printed his version of Aeschylus' *Agamemnon.* The indignation of the critics can be imagined when in 1880 and 1881 he published Sophocles' *Oedipus Tyrannus* and *Oedipus Coloneus* telescoped into a single drama.

His interest in Oriental literature had been initiated by his boyhood friend, Major Moor, and had been nourished on the idea that the etymology of *Erin* (his ancestral home) and *Iran* were related. Cowell quickly disabused him of this when he began studying with him in 1852. Four years later, he had completed his translation of Jámí's *Salámán and Absál* in Miltonic blank verse. Because of his admission of his free mode of translation, critics who could not read the original reviewed most harshly what he always considered to be his masterpiece.

In 1856 FitzGerald first encountered the work which was destined to secure him literary and popular fame. Cowell discovered at the Bodleian

Library, Oxford University, a manuscript of a little known Persian poem, the *Rubáiyát* of Omar Khayyám. He copied it and sent it to FitzGerald, and they began to read it together. Cowell then discovered a second manuscript at the Library of the Bengal Asiatic Society at Calcutta and sent him a copy of that. First FitzGerald tried translating it into Latin. Within six months after receiving the Calcutta copy, the poet had translated most of the "quatrains" into English and sent them to *Frazer's Magazine*. When they were held for a year, he recalled them, added 40 more stanzas, and printed 250 copies in plain brown-paper covers at his own expense, sending about 200 to Bernard Quaritch, the bookseller. Sales moved so slowly that Quaritch put them into the discards, on the penny stand. Here they were discovered by friends of Dante Gabriel Rossetti, who in turn told Swinburne. They spread the word, but the reviewers ignored the poem. It first achieved fame in the United States, when it was praised by Charles Eliot Norton. There too, Mrs. Sarah Wister, Fanny Kemble's daughter, first identified FitzGerald as the anonymous author. A new edition was soon demanded, and the translator expanded his original 75 quatrains to 110. By the end of the century it had appeared in five versions and been printed in countless editions, translated into many languages, including both Latin and Erse, and had profoundly influenced the thinking of a generation.

FitzGerald then turned to the *Bird Parliament*, which he translated from the *Mantiq ut-Tair* of the Persian Farid ud-din Attár, and published in 1889. This is a sort of birds' *Pilgrim's Progress*.

FitzGerald had a clear vision of his own principles of both literary criticism and personal life, and was often uncomfortably perceptive. It is true that his judgments, unflinchingly made known to stranger and friend, were limited by the tastes of his youth, but they were based in a sense of fine craftsmanship. He loved the ancient Greeks, Shakespeare, Scott, and Tennyson at his prime. He never wholly liked Wordsworth, and had a distaste for all the Pre-Raphaelites, however they might praise him. He detested the sentimentality of Mrs. Browning and what he considered the barbarity of her husband.

He had a clear vision of what he wanted for himself—not wealth and fame, but a quiet life with a few friends; a small private refuge of a house; his books, music, and paintings; the tang of sea spray in his nostrils, and the sight of blossoms and birds in the meadow. Although he always had more than enough money, his own life was abstemious, and he was a vegetarian, eating meat only in public so as not to be considered eccentric. He had contempt for ostentation and selfishness, and a profound respect for the hardy English peasant and seaman. He had a strong sense of social responsibility too. He regularly paid a doctor to attend the poor. He fought rigorously against injustice and mistreatment of man and beast.

The passing years did not deal kindly with the poet. His father had died in bankruptcy; his mother passed away; in the fifties alone he lost four of his dearest friends. He was haunted by the failure of his marriage. Ultimately he withdrew from London because he felt it was inhabited by a "decayed race," and equally from local Woodbridge society with its selfishness and pride. He was disappointed in Posh. His failing eyesight drove him from his boating expeditions and forced him to rely upon incompetent readers. His six feet of height became stooped, his side-beards and the fringe of whiskers beneath his chin became gray. The townspeople of Woodbridge laughed at his worn clothes (though he had better), at his short trousers, and his cape flying in the wind as he ambled down the road, his slouch hat tied on with a kerchief.

He was at his best in letters to the friends he kept for a lifetime, or when he was with them, for they often gathered together at his house or he visited them, even on occasion in London. Mrs. Donne wrote, "He is a most agreeable person, laughter-loving and ever suited to make holiday. The children think so too and spare him not." His friend from college days, Alfred Lord Tennyson, remembered him as one

> Whom yet I see as there you sit
>   Beneath your sheltering garden-tree
> And watch your doves about you flit,
>   And plant on shoulder, hand and knee,
>   Or on your head their rosy feet. . . .
>
> . . . recalling gracious times,
>   When, in our younger London days,
> You found some merit in my rhymes,
>   And I more pleasure in your praise.[3]

Finally, he passed away quietly in his sleep while on a visit to his friend Rev. Crabbe at Merton.

3. Tennyson, Alfred Lord, "To E. FitzGerald," *Tiresias and Other Poems.* London, Macmillan and Co., 1885.

A CREATIVE TRANSLATION

It is often said that the *Rubáiyát* is more the work of FitzGerald than of Omar. This is not true, although FitzGerald himself is partly responsible for the misconception. He always felt that a translation could not be both literal and yet retain the spirit of the original. In the ideal translation, he maintained, the translator must be a perfect poet able to re-create in his own language and for his own people the true spirit of the original. Because each language has its own special constructions, cadences, and style of imagery, to say nothing of meaning which reflects the whole attitude and history of the people, such a reincarnation of a poem written almost a millennium ago and almost half a world away is always difficult. FitzGerald therefore did not hesitate to edit or to recast the language in the idiom and philosophy he considered equivalent in his own time. With conscious integrity, he invariably stated in prefaces to his translations, whether from Spanish, Greek, or Persian, that he had made such alterations. The critics, who too often could not read the original or did not make the effort to do so, were horrified at what they considered barbaric license. Further, the differences between FitzGerald's versions of the *Rubáiyát,* especially in the very first stanza, heighten the impression of an extraordinarily free rendering of the original. The idea is confirmed by the fact that the first version has only 75 quatrains while the second, for example, has 110. However, not a single one of the greatest translations in English has been literal.

Actually, however, FitzGerald has not seriously abused the privilege of a translator whose intention is primarily literary rather than scholarly. For the first version he used as sources Ouseley Manuscript 140 in the Bodleian Library, Oxford, consisting of 158 stanzas, and the Calcutta manuscript of 516 stanzas, both sent him by Cowell. In addition, for the second, he had recourse to the literal French translation by J. B. Nicolas from a lithograph copy consisting of 464 rubáiyát, which was discovered at Teheran. The problem has been closely studied by Edward Heron-Allen.[4] He points out:

> Of Edward FitzGerald's quatrains, forty-nine are faithful and beautiful paraphrases of single quatrains to be found in the Ouseley or Calcutta MSS or both.
>
> Forty-four are traceable to more than one quatrain and may therefore be termed the "Composite" quatrains.
>
> Two are inspired by quatrains found by Fitz-Gerald only in Nicolas' text. (46 and 98)
>
> Two are quatrains reflecting the whole spirit of the original poem. (5 and 86)

4. Heron-Allen, Edward, *Rubá'iyát of 'Umar Khayyám.* London, Duckworth & Co., 1908, pp. xi-xii.

23

Two are traceable exclusively to the influence of the Mantik ut-tair of Ferid-ud din Attár. (33 and 34)

Two quatrains primarily inspired by Omar were influenced by the Odes of Hafiz. (2 and 3)

Thus he accounts for 101 stanzas of the poem in final form. There is no question that, while Nicolas and Whinfield translate each quatrain more exactly, FitzGerald is often as accurate and unquestionably more vital and poetic.

The original order of the quatrains is not logical but alphabetical according to the final letter of the rhyming word of each. Since FitzGerald could hardly convey this satisfactorily in English and, since meaning is more essential, he decided to arrange the stanzas in a sequence which reflects both the progress of the day from dawn to dusk and a development of mood. As he says in a letter to his bookseller, Bernard Quaritch, "He begins with Dawn, pretty sober & contemplative: then as he thinks and drinks, grows savage, blasphemous, etc., and then again sobers down into melancholy at nightfall." The revisions in later versions do not violate these principles.

FitzGerald of course also changed the language of the translation in successive versions, the first and second being generally closer to the original. However, three stanzas contained in them and not found in any original text were omitted by Fitz-Gerald in the later versions. His reasons for change are interesting. For example, the famous opening stanza of the first version was changed because he had used a similar image in translating Jámí's

Salámán and Absál. He sought always a more exact or musical word, tried to improve the rhythm, and to use a clearer or more vivid figure of speech. Whether he succeeded may be open to question. He himself wrote Quaritch, "I daresay Ed[n] 1 is better in some respects than 2, but I think not altogether. . . . As to the relative fidelity of the two Versions, there isn't a Pin to choose. . . ."

The title of the poem might best be translated as "quatrains." It is in the form which was commonly employed for Persian epigrammatic verse. Actually, a *rubái* is a two-line stanza, the line (called a *bayt*) being six or eight feet in length. Each line is divided into halves called *misrá*. Of the four half-lines usually the first, second, and fourth rhyme (*aaba*), and the third is not only unrhymed but can vary in length. FitzGerald regularized the structure and created quatrains of iambic pentameter, imitating the Persian rhyme scheme. This creation has since been called the "FitzGerald stanza" and has been employed by several poets since, most notably (with some variations) by Swinburne in his "Laus Veneris" and his elegy on Gautier. The translator describes the effect at the conclusion to his preface to the first edition thus: "The original Rubáiyát . . . are independent Stanzas, consisting each of four Lines of equal, though varied, Prosody, sometimes *all* rhyming, but oftener (as here attempted) the third line suspending the Cadence by which the last atones with the former Two. Something as in the Greek Alcaic, where the third line seems to lift and suspend the Wave that falls over in the last."

More essential are the changes in philosophy. In

general Omar's original poem gives one an impression of greater freedom, cheerfulness, and broad-mindedness, while FitzGerald reflects less concern with physical love and greater Victorian preoccupation with death and life hereafter. Nevertheless, the translator found in his original a spiritual companionship—a mixture of earthly pleasure and self-indulgence, and yet an intellectual resentment that He who created beauty and man to enjoy it should yet have trapped him in mortality and moral responsibility. It reflected superbly the spiritual dilemma and refuge of both the eleventh-century Persian poet and his nineteenth-century English translator. So effective was the translation that it helped to voice and to determine the melancholy sensuousness and spiritual doubt of the last half of the nineteenth century in England.

THE TEXTS

For purposes of this edition, the first of the five versions prepared by FitzGerald has been used as the basic text. The fifth and final version has been included for purposes of comparison and to enable the reader to select his favorite form of a given quatrain, as each reader will have his special preferences. For example, it has generally been agreed that the first form of the first stanza is the best. But the twelfth quatrain did not achieve its most memorable form until the third version. Who does not prefer "Ah, Take the Cash, and let the Credit go" to "Ah, take the Cash in hand and waive the Rest"? The author wrote to his publisher, "I daresay Ed^n 1 is better in some respects than 2, but I think not altogether. . . . I dare say Ed^n 1 best pleased those who read it first: as first Impressions are apt to be strongest. . . ." This has proved to be the case.

There has been much analysis of FitzGerald's method of translating and rationale of revision, most notably in the work of Heron-Allen and Arberry, cited in the bibliography, to which the reader is referred. It will be noted in comparing the versions that the first comprised 75 quatrains. Upon consulting Nicolas's French text, the author increased the second version to 110. Nine stanzas were omitted and never employed again in the remaining versions, so that the number was reduced to 101. As we trace the changes FitzGerald made, we note that not only were quatrains added or omitted, but lines were compressed and often images and meanings were clarified and strengthened. However, as the first quatrain demonstrates, all changes were not for the better.

FitzGerald made a free paraphrase of Omar, although almost every English quatrain can be traced to a Persian original. The English writer himself wrote to Quaritch that, "As to the relative fidelity of the two Versions, there isn't a Pin to choose. . . ." However, we can now observe generally that, as he reworked the material, he often departed further and further from the original, as in Stanza I (all editions) and XI (first edition, XII in subsequent versions). Revisions can be most conveniently appreciated by reference to the *Comparative Table* on p. 127, as developed by Edward Heron-Allen.

Often the later versions clarified the imagery. Thus in the first version, Stanza II opens with "Dreaming when Dawn's Left Hand was in the Sky," but the third says, "Before the phantom of False morning died." On the other hand, one might prefer the last two lines of Quatrain V in the first version:

> But still the Vine her ancient Ruby yields,
> And still a Garden by the Water blows.

For this, the third version gives:

> But still a Ruby kindles in the Vine
> And many a Garden by the Water blows.

Yet *kindles* has a more dynamic quality than *yields*. So one might analyze stanza after stanza, and conclude that each version has some special beauty.

In the original, each *rubái* is a separate poem. The various manuscripts do not establish any special order. The arrangement was FitzGerald's contribution, and he operated according to the scheme described on p. 24. He therefore felt perfectly free to rearrange the stanzas in each edition as he pleased. Thus Stanza LX in the first edition is XCIV in the second and LXXXVII in the third, fourth, and fifth.

Because we believe that each reader will find something to please him in each version, we have included with FitzGerald's first effort his final thought as expressed in the fifth version. A comparison will be illuminating.

RUBÁIYÁT
of
OMAR KHAYYÁM

TRANSLATED BY
EDWARD FITZGERALD

(First Version)

1. In the desert, flinging a stone into a cup is a signal to mount horse.

2. *Dawn's Left Hand.* The false dawn which precedes true dawn by about an hour.

3. *Life's Liquor.* Wine is often regarded as the symbol of life. However, the drinking of alcoholic beverages is forbidden to Mohammedans. To the Súfis, wine represented love for God, and drunkenness signified religious fervor. However, it is questionable whether Omar was a Súfi and intended the latter meanings.

4. *Cock crew.* The crowing of the cock not only ushers in the day but dispels the evil phantoms of night. Those who beg entrance to the Tavern are not just tipplers but, since the Tavern symbolizes life itself, they are seeking to make the most of life from its very beginning.

I

Awake! for Morning in the Bowl of Night
Has flung the Stone [1] that puts the Stars to Flight:
   And Lo! the Hunter of the East has caught
The Sultán's Turret in a Noose of Light.

II

Dreaming when Dawn's Left Hand [2] was in the Sky
I heard a Voice within the Tavern cry,
   "Awake, my Little ones, and fill the Cup
Before Life's Liquor [3] in its Cup be dry."

III

And, as the Cock crew,[4] those who stood before
The Tavern shouted—"Open then the Door.
   You know how little while we have to stay,
And, once departed, may return no more."

5. *New Year*. The Persians began the new year with spring, at the vernal equinox.

6. *WHITE HAND OF MOSES*. In Exodus IV, 6, God is instructing Moses in the miracles he is to perform before Pharaoh. When he takes his hand out of his bosom, it is "leprous, as white as snow." Here the comparison is to the white blossoms of spring.

7. *Jesus from the Ground suspires*. Mohammedans believe that the healing power of Jesus is in his breath. According to the Koran, Sura V. 110, Jesus breathed into the clay and turned it into the "likeness of a bird."

8. *Irám* (Ee'-ram). A legendary city of ancient Arabia, supposed to have been established by Shaddád bin 'Ad. It was adorned with jewels and famous for its marvelous gardens. It became the metaphor for Paradise.

9. *Jamshyd's Sev'n-ring'd Cup* (Jam'-sheed). Jamshyd was the most celebrated king of the legendary Peeshdádian dynasty and, according to Firdausî, reigned for 700 years. His magical cup had seven rings, symbolic of the seven heavens, seven planets, seven seas, and the like.

10. *Pélevi* (Pel'-e-vee). Sanskrit, the ancient language of Persia and India.

11. *Yellow* in Persian literature represents sickness or misery.

IV

Now the New Year [5] reviving old Desires,
The thoughtful Soul to Solitude retires,
   Where the WHITE HAND OF MOSES [6] on the
     Bough
Puts out, and Jesus from the Ground suspires.[7]

V

Irám [8] indeed is gone with all its Rose,
And Jamshyd's Sev'n-ring'd Cup [9] where no one
     knows;
   But still the Vine her ancient Ruby yields,
And still a Garden by the Water blows.

VI

And David's Lips are lock't; but in divine
High piping, Pélevi,[10] with "Wine! Wine! Wine!
   Red Wine!"—the Nightingale cries to the Rose
That yellow [11] Cheek of hers to'incarnadine.

12. O. Henry, in "The Rubáiyát of a Scotch Highball," in *The Trimmed Lamp*, tells the story of a man and wife who love the *Rubáiyát* and have become addicted to drink. When the husband decides to break the habit, he recites this quatrain.

13. *Kaikobád* (Kye'-ko-bahd). A mythical king of ancient Persia.

14. *Kaikhosrú* (Kye'-kos-roo). The Persian name for Cyrus, founder of the Persian dynasty.

15. *Rustum* is the Persian Hercules of the Shah-náma. One of his tragic exploits is recounted in Matthew Arnold's famous poem, *Sohrab and Rustum*.

16. *Hátim Tai* (Hah'-tim Tye). A mythical Persian king famed for his generosity.

VII

Come, fill the Cup, and in the Fire of Spring
The Winter Garment of Repentance fling:
  The Bird of Time has but a little way
To fly—and Lo! the Bird is on the Wing.[12]

VIII

And look—a thousand Blossoms with the Day
Woke—and a thousand scatter'd into Clay:
  And this first Summer Month that brings the
    Rose
Shall take Jamshyd and Kaikobád [13] away.

IX

But come with old Khayyám, and leave the Lot
Of Kaikobád and Kaikhosrú [14] forgot:
  Let Rustum [15] lay about him as he will,
Or Hátim Tai [16] cry Supper—heed them not.

17. *Desert.* According to the Súfis, the desert represents the pure life in which the lovers of God must live if they are to cleanse the soul of desire for earthly things such as wealth, fame, and pleasure. However, Omar probably intended the oasis in the desert merely as an island of refuge from the cares of life and man's obsession with mortality.

18. *Sultán Máhmúd* (Sul'-tan Mah'-mud). Máhmúd of Ghazna, whose name is derived from Mohammed and means "the praised," conquered northern India and is celebrated in Persian poetry. His passion for his slave-boy Ayáz is used by Persian poets to demonstrate how unpredictable love can be.

19. *Paradise.* The Súfis used Paradise to represent attraction to the pleasures of this world.

20. *Ah, take the Cash in hand and waive the Rest.* This line was vastly improved in later versions, in which form it has become better known. Compare with the Fifth Version, Quatrain XIII, line 3.

X

With me along some Strip of Herbage strown
That just divides the desert [17] from the sown,
  Where name of Slave and Sultán scarce is
    known,
And pity Sultán Máhmúd [18] on his Throne.

XI

Here with a Loaf of Bread beneath the Bough,
A Flask of Wine, a Book of Verse—and Thou
  Beside me singing in the Wilderness—
And Wilderness is Paradise [19] enow.

XII

"How sweet is mortal Sovranty!"—think some:
Others—"How blest the Paradise to come!"
  Ah, take the Cash in hand and waive the Rest; [20]
Oh, the brave Music of a *distant* Drum!

21. *Rose.* This flower is referred to often in this work. What
do you judge it symbolizes?

22. *Ashes. Snow.* Note that both of these are white, but
have opposing significance.

23. *Buried once.* In the East, treasure is buried at night
when an attack of robbers is expected.

XIII

Look to the Rose [21] that blows about us—"Lo,
Laughing," she says, "into the World I blow:
  At once the silken Tassel of my Purse
Tear, and its Treasure on the Garden throw."

XIV

The Worldly Hope men set their Hearts upon
Turns Ashes [22]—or it prospers; and anon,
  Like Snow [22] upon the Desert's dusty Face
Lighting a little Hour or two—is gone.

XV

And those who husbanded the Golden Grain,
And those who flung it to the Winds like Rain,
  Alike to no such aureate Earth are turn'd
As, buried once, [23] Men want dug up again.

24. *Caravanserai.* An inn where caravans stop for the night.

25. *Courts where Jamshyd gloried* (Jam'-sheed). This mythical Persian king is supposed by some to have built the beautiful palace at Persepolis, referred to here. Others say it was constructed by Ján ibn Ján, who they claim built the Egyptian pyramids before the time of Adam.

26. *Bahrám* Gur (Bah'-ram goor), or "Bahram of the Wild Ass" (from his skill in hunting the animal) was a Sassanian king who ruled A.D. 420-438. He had seven castles, each of a different color.

    Robert Browning misquoted these lines in a letter of October 22, 1889, to George Barrett, as "The wild ass o'er her head / Stamps with his foot and nought disturbs her sleep." This was cited in the course of a furious resentment at FitzGerald for a slight directed at Browning's recently deceased wife, Elizabeth Barrett Browning, the poetess. FitzGerald's letters had just been published by William Aldis Wright and, in a letter to W. H. Thompson (Wright, I, pp. 280-1), FitzGerald had written, "Mrs. Browning's death is rather a relief to me," for he detested her poem "Aurora Leigh."

27. This stanza is noteworthy for its evocation of color and a satiating perfume. Compare it with a similar expression of the same idea in Edna St. Vincent Millay's "Renascence."

XVI

Think, in this batter'd Caravanserai [24]
Whose Doorways are alternate Night and Day,
   How Sultán after Sultán with his Pomp
Abode his Hour or two, and went his way.

XVII

They say the Lion and the Lizard keep
The Courts where Jamshyd gloried [25] and drank
   deep:
   And Bahrám,[26] that great Hunter—the Wild Ass
Stamps o'er his Head, and he lies fast asleep.

XVIII

I sometimes think that never blows so red
The Rose as where some buried Cæsar bled;
   That every Hyacinth the Garden wears
Dropt in its Lap from some once lovely Head.[27]

28. *Lip*. Note the play on the word in this quatrain, as well as in Quatrains XXXIV, XXXV, and XLVII.

29. *Sev'n Thousand Years*. The number *seven* has a mystic significance. See Quatrain V and its note. In what other common expressions is the number used?

30. Compare this stanza with Quatrain XXII of the Fifth Version and note how it has been clarified.

XIX

And this delightful Herb whose tender Green
Fledges the River's Lip [28] on which we lean—
   Ah, lean upon it lightly! for who knows
From what once lovely Lip [28] it springs unseen!

XX

Ah! my Belovéd, fill the Cup that clears
To-DAY of past Regrets and future Fears—
   To-morrow?—Why, To-morrow I may be
Myself with Yesterday's Sev'n Thousand Years.[29]

XXI

Lo! some we loved, the loveliest and the best
That Time and Fate of all their Vintage prest,
   Have drunk their Cup a Round or two before
And one by one crept silently to Rest.[30]

31. *Couch.* Themes are interwoven throughout the poem. Note how this has been prepared for by Quatrain XIX.

32. *Dust.* This is a common Biblical theme. Cf. Genesis III, 19; Job X, 9 and XXXIV, 15; and Ecclesiastes III, 20 and XII, 7.

33. *Muezzín* (mew-ez'-zin). A crier who, from the top of the minaret of a mosque, calls the faithful to prayer five times a day. This is not in Omar's original.

XXII

And we, that now make merry in the Room
They left, and Summer dresses in new Bloom,
   Ourselves must we beneath the Couch [31] of Earth
Descend, ourselves to make a Couch—for whom?

XXIII

Ah, make the most of what we yet may spend,
Before we too into the Dust [32] Descend;
   Dust into Dust, and under Dust, to lie,
Sans Wine, sans Song, sans Singer and—sans End!

XXIV

Alike for those who for TO-DAY prepare,
And those that after a TO-MORROW stare,
   A Muezzín [33] from the Tower of Darkness cries
"Fools! your Reward is neither Here nor There."

34. *Discuss'd . . . Words . . . Mouths.* Note how this theme is developed within the quatrain, making it a coherent unit, building to its climactic, pessimistic statement.

35. In later versions this quatrain was slightly modified, and made more vehement, so that FitzGerald in the fifth version makes it Quatrain LXIII in accordance with his general plan of increasing bitterness as the "day" embraced by the poem wore on.

36. *Door.* The word "frequent" in the first line suggests entrance to a building and thus a physical door. In the fourth line this idea is given a symbolic meaning.

XXV

Why, all the Saints and Sages who discuss'd
Of the Two Worlds so learnedly, are thrust
   Like foolish Prophets forth; their Words to
     Scorn
Are scatter'd, and their Mouths [34] are stopt with
     Dust.

XXVI

Oh, come with old Khayyám, and leave the Wise
To talk; one thing is certain, that Life flies;
   One thing is certain, and the Rest is Lies;
The Flower that once has blown for ever dies.[35]

XXVII

Myself when young did eagerly frequent
Doctor and Saint, and heard great Argument
   About it and about: but evermore
Came out by the same Door [36] as in I went.

37. The fluid images of the last line intensify the vanity of his attempt to find real wisdom with "Doctor and Saint." Compare Ecclesiastes I, 6-7, 14, 17; II, 11 for imagery, but note the difference in idea in IX, 13-18.

38. In this stanza, FitzGerald makes extensive use of alliteration on *w* together with the nasal *n* and liquid *l*. The effect dramatizes his idea. Compare this with the following quatrain.

39. Observe the effectiveness of the play of alliteration on *w* and *h* in suggesting the force of the wind hurling insubstantial man to his destiny, as well as haste and breathlessness. The final two lines stop the current with their gesture of defiance.

XXVIII

With them the Seed of Wisdom did I sow,
And with my own hand labour'd it to grow:
   And this was all the Harvest that I reap'd—
"I came like Water, and like Wind I go." [37]

XXIX

Into this Universe, and *why* not knowing,
Nor *whence*, like Water willy-nilly flowing:
   And out of it, as Wind along the Waste,
I know not *whither*, willy-nilly blowing. [38]

XXX

What, without asking, hither hurried *whence*?
And, without asking, *whither* hurried hence! [39]
   Another and another Cup to drown
The Memory of this Impertinence!

40. *Seventh Gate . . . Throne of Saturn.* Saturn rules the
seventh heaven because it is sixth in order from the sun,
which rules the first.

41. John Ruskin quoted this as "such a jolly stanza" out of
a "delightful Eastern poem," when he first read the
Rubáiyát (Letter, September 27, 1863, to Mrs. John
Simon). He took strong objection to the idea expressed
in Quatrain XXXIV, but agreed with equal vigor with
Quatrains XXI, XXV, XLV, and XLVI.

42. *ME and THEE.* The *Door* and *Veil* may be those of
death or those which obscure the answer to the riddle
of existence. Therefore, *ME and THEE* may mean that
after our brief lives there is no more concern for us.
It may mean also that man is very unimportant in the
vastness of the universe. The Súfis would say that death
frees man from selfishness and permits him to become
united with God.

43. Compare this stanza with its equivalent, Quatrain XXXIV
in the Fifth Version. The clear irony of the First Version
has been considerably obscured. FitzGerald did not
always improve his work with revision, the most notable
example being the first stanza.

XXXI

Up from Earth's Centre through the seventh Gate
I rose, and on the Throne of Saturn [40] sate;
    And many Knots unravel'd by the Road;
But not the Knot of Human Death and Fate.

XXXII [41]

There was a Door to which I found no Key:
There was a veil past which I could not see:
    Some little Talk awhile of ME and THEE [42]
There seemed—and then no more of THEE and ME.

XXXIII

Then to the rolling Heav'n itself I cried,
Asking, "What Lamp had Destiny to guide
    Her little Children stumbling in the Dark?"
And—"A blind understanding!" Heav'n replied. [43]

44. *Secret Well of Life.* This was later revised to read *Secret of my Life.* In Omar's original, this *secret* is defined as length of life.

45. The artistry of the English poet is clearly revealed in the compression and unity of this stanza, with its references to *articulation, Lip,* and *Kisses.* Omar's original refers also to an unlucky lover, the hair, and the throat of the beloved, as well as the hand of the lover.

46. *Potter.* The comparison of the *pot* and *potter* to *man* and his *Maker* is common in literature from the Hebrew prophets to the present, e.g., "Hath not the potter power over the clay, of the same lump to make one vessel unto honour, and another unto dishonour." Romans IX, 21. See also Jeremiah XVIII, 1-6.

XXXIV

Then to this earthen Bowl did I adjourn
My Lip the secret Well of Life [44] to learn:
  And Lip to Lip it murmur'd—"While you live,
Drink!—for once dead you never shall return."

XXXV

I think the Vessel, that with fugitive
Articulation answer'd, once did live,
  And merry-make; and the cold Lip I kiss'd
How many Kisses [45] might it take—and give.

XXXVI

For in the Market-place, one Dusk of Day,
I watch'd the Potter [46] thumping his wet Clay:
  And with its all obliterated Tongue
It murmur'd—"Gently, Brother, gently, pray!"

47. *The Stars are setting* . . . Apparently the Caravan is traveling by night to avoid the heat of the day.

48. Stanza XLII of the Fifth Version shows a complete change of philosophy, revealing a sense of eternity in time rather than the transience of life here expressed. The first version is closer to Omar.

49. *Grape* . . . *Fruit.* In keeping with the theme of the vanity of mortal ambitions, the *fruitful Grape* is contrasted with joys totally missed or embittered—a sort of progression of idea and evanescence of the senses of which FitzGerald is very fond.

XXXVII

One Moment in Annihilation's Waste,
One moment, of the Well of Life to taste—
  The Stars are setting,[47] and the Caravan
Starts for the dawn of Nothing—Oh, make haste!

XXXVIII

Ah, fill the Cup:—what boots it to repeat
How Time is slipping underneath our Feet:
  Unborn TO-MORROW and dead YESTERDAY,
Why fret about them if TO-DAY be sweet! [48]

XXXIX

How long, how long, in infinite Pursuit
Of This and That endeavour and dispute?
  Better be merry with the fruitful Grape [49]
Than sadden after none, or bitter, Fruit.

50. *Marriage . . . Divorced old barren Reason.* FitzGerald's abortive attempt at marriage took place in 1856, the year in which he began his study of the *Rubáiyát*. The poet married Lucy Barton to gratify her dying father's wish. She was 48, a cultured, benevolent woman, but big-boned, with heavy features and a loud voice, ardently religious and ambitious for social advancement. They were hopelessly incompatible and separated after a few months. He turned from her to his former carefree bachelor life. This may be the origin of these lines.

51. *Rule and Line.* Whereas Omar was a famous mathematician, FitzGerald was lamentably weak in that area of study.

52. This is a mistranslation from the Persian, in which the original means "old man."

XL

You know, my Friends, how long since in my
   House
For a new Marriage I did make Carouse:
   Divorced old barren Reason from my Bed,[50]
And took the Daughter of the Vine to Spouse.

XLI

For "Is" and "Is-not" though *with* Rule and Line,[51]
And, "Up-and-Down" *without,* I could define,
   I yet in all I only cared to know,
Was never deep in anything but—Wine.

XLII

And lately, by the Tavern Door agape,
Came stealing through the Dusk an Angel Shape,[52]
   Bearing a vessel on his Shoulder; and
He bid me taste of it; and 'twas—the Grape!

53. *Two-and-Seventy jarring Sects.* Islamism was split into 72 fiercely quarreling sects, involved in unending dispute.

54. *Misbelieving and black Horde.* Mahmúd the Great (see note on Quatrain X) had conquered northern India and its dark-skinned idol worshipers. The reference is based on a passage in the *Mantiq ut-Tair* of Farid ud-din Attár, which FitzGerald had studied.

55. So widely read was the *Rubáiyát* even in the American West, that the Hon. John Hay, speaking before the Omar Khayyám Club of London, December 8, 1897, said that in the Rocky Mountains a frontiersman was heard to quote this stanza.

XLIII

The Grape that can with Logic absolute
The Two-and-Seventy jarring Sects [53] confute:
   The subtle Alchemist that in a Trice
Life's leaden Metal into Gold transmute.

XLIV

The mighty Mahmúd, the victorious Lord,
That all the misbelieving and black Horde [54]
   Of Fears and Sorrows that infest the Soul
Scatters and slays with his enchanted Sword.

XLV

But leave the Wise to wrangle, and with me
The Quarrel of the Universe let be:
   And, in some corner of the Hubbub coucht,
Make Game of that which makes as much of
   Thee.[55]

56. *Magic Shadow-show.* This is the *fanúsi khiyál,* a lantern
    which has figures painted inside a cylinder and is cut
    with slits and so delicately balanced that it revolves with
    the heat of the lighted candle inside. Compare this with
    the kinetoscope, ancestor of the motion-picture projector,
    and with a modern child's bedroom lamp with revolving
    shade. Note the similarity to Plato's famous simile.

57. Compare this stanza with XXXVIII, and then with XLII
    of the Fifth Version to discover the great variations
    FitzGerald played on the original theme, most accurately
    translated in XXXVIII of the First Version.

58. *Angel with his darker Draught.* Azrael, the angel of
    death, is here pictured as offering man the drink of
    death. In one Oriental legend, he holds to man's nostrils
    an apple from the Tree of Life.

XLVI

For in and out, above, about, below,
'Tis nothing but a Magic Shadow-show,[56]
   Play'd in a Box whose Candle is the Sun,
Round which we Phantom Figures come and go.

XLVII

And if the Wine you drink, the Lip you press,
End in the Nothing all Things end in—Yes—
   Then fancy while Thou art, Thou art but what
Thou shalt be—Nothing—Thou shalt not be less.[57]

XLVIII

While the Rose blows along the River Brink,
With old Khayyám the Ruby Vintage drink:
   And when the Angel with his darker Draught[58]
Draws up to thee—take that, and do not shrink.

59. *Chequer-board.* The reference here is to the game of chess. Games are the source of several images in the poem. What are they? What is their significance?

60. *Ball.* The game of polo is the source of this metaphor.

61. Compare with the Bible, Daniel V.

XLIX

'Tis all a Chequer-board [59] of Nights and Days
Where Destiny with Men for Pieces plays:
  Hither and thither moves, and mates, and slays,
And one by one back in the Closet lays.

L

The Ball [60] no Question makes of Ayes and Noes,
But Right or Left as strikes the Player goes;
  And He that toss'd Thee down into the Field,
He knows about it all—HE knows—HE knows!

LI

The Moving Finger writes; [61] and, having writ,
Moves on: nor all thy Piety nor Wit
  Shall lure it back to cancel half a Line,
Nor all thy Tears wash out a Word of it.

62. *Lift not thy hands . . . Thou or I.* D. H. Lawrence, the
modern novelist and poet, in *The Chambers Papers*, p.
593, says, "I thrilled with the daring of Omar Khayyám:
> 'Lift not thy hands to It for help—for It
> Rolls impotently on as Thou or I.'
My mother didn't like our discussing the *Rubáiyát* before the young children: 'I won't have their faith
destroyed. You grieve me by reading such things, but
you shan't take the children's faith.'"

63. *First Morning of Creation . . . Last Dawn of Reckoning.*
Note the extreme contrast of the two dawns. Is the
Reckoning inconsistent with the general theme of pre-
destination expressed here?

64. *Foal.* The following stars are in the neck of the constella-
tion Taurus the Bull.

65. *Parwín* (pahr'-win). The Pleiades.

66. *Mushtarí* (mush'-tah-ree). The planet Jupiter.

LII

And that inverted Bowl we call The Sky,
Whereunder crawling coop't we live and die,
   Lift not thy hands to *It* for help—for It
Rolls impotently on as Thou or I.[62]

LIII

With Earth's first Clay They did the Last Man's
  · knead,
And then of the Last Harvest sow'd the Seed:
   Yea, the first Morning of Creation wrote
What the Last Dawn of Reckoning [63] shall read.

LIV

I tell Thee this—When, starting from the Goal,
Over the shoulders of the flaming Foal [64]
   Of Heav'n Parwín [65] and Mushtarí [66] they flung,
In my predestin'd Plot of Dust and Soul.

67. *Súfi* (soo'-fi). Mohammedan mystics, pantheists, forced into employing symbolism because their beliefs were considered heretical by orthodox Mohammedans. See p. 11.

In Omar's original, the key unlocks the "treasures of the pearl of Meaning" (Arberry).

68. *True Light.* If this expression were contained in Omar's original (which it is not), it would have a very different meaning to orthodox Moslem, Súfi, or Christian. This stanza does not express the attitude of an irreligious man, but rather of one endlessly seeking answers to the most profound religious and moral questions wherever he can.

69. *Gin.* Trap or snare for wild game.

70. Compare this quatrain with LIII and LIV.

LV

The Vine had struck a Fibre; which about
It clings my Being—let the Súfi [67] flout;
   Of my Base Metal may be filed a Key,
That shall unlock the Door he howls without.

LVI

And this I know: whether the one True Light, [68]
Kindle to Love, or Wrath consume me quite,
   One Glimpse of It within the Tavern caught
Better than in the Temple lost outright.

LVII

Oh Thou who didst with Pitfall and with Gin [69]
Beset the Road I was to wander in,
   Thou wilt not with Predestination round
Enmesh me, and impute my Fall to Sin? [70]

71. *Snake.* William Aldis Wright considers FitzGerald here
to have mistranslated the original, but there is no question that the English is harmonious with the general
philosophy expressed. A similar reference is found in the
Mantiq ut-Tàir, with which FitzGerald was very familiar.
Mark Twain regarded this stanza "as containing the
most far-reaching and grand thought ever expressed in
so short a space, in so few words." Evelyn Hardy reports that, just before he died, Thomas Hardy, the great
modern novelist, dramatist, and poet, asked that this
stanza be read to him.

72. *KUZA—NÁMA* (koo'-za nah'-mà). "Book of pots," the
title given to stanzas LIX to LXVI in this version.

73. *Ramazán* (ram'-a-zan). Ramadan, the ninth month of
the Mohammedan year, during which strict fasting is
required. Literally, the "hot month." The "better Moon"
will rise when the Ramadan is over and the fast con-
cluded.

74. *One more impatient.* In later versions, FitzGerald rede-
fined this as *a Súfi pipkin.* The earlier form is closer to
the original. The purpose of the next line seems to be a
satire on philosophical confusion, which confounds one
thing with another.

LVIII

Oh Thou, who Man of baser Earth didst make,
And who with Eden didst devise the Snake;[71]
  For all the Sin wherewith the Face of Man
Is blacken'd, Man's Forgiveness give—and take!

✳ ✳ ✳ ✳ ✳

LIX

KUZA—NÁMA [72]

Listen again. One Evening at the Close
Of Ramazán,[73] ere the better Moon arose,
  In that old Potter's Shop I stood alone
With the clay Population round in Rows.

LX

And strange to tell, among that Earthen Lot
Some could articulate, while others not:
  And suddenly one more impatient [74] cried—
"Who *is* the Potter, pray, and who the Pot?"

75. *Common Earth*. The contrast between this repeated expression and *Shape* symbolizes the antithesis of chaos and order, made the more effective by *Shape* being placed in the unrhymed line. The satire here is of a common mode of religious reasoning.

76. *Shall He that made . . . destroy*! This is a mistranslation of Omar's original, in which he asks *for whom* the Creator makes and destroys.

77. In this quatrain FitzGerald pushes to a limit the ideas of an Omnipotent Creator and predestination, with an unexpected sense of pathos. Compare this with Quatrains LVII and LVIII.

LXI

Then said another—"Surely not in vain
My substance from the common Earth was ta'en,
    That He who subtly wrought me into Shape
Should stamp me back to common Earth [75] again."

LXII

Another said—"Why, ne'er a peevish Boy
Would break the Bowl from which he drank in
        Joy;
    Shall He that *made* the Vessel in pure Love
And Fancy, in an after Rage destroy!" [76]

LXIII

None answer'd this; but after Silence spake
A Vessel of a more ungainly Make:
    "They sneer at me for leaning all awry;
What? did the Hand then of the Potter shake?" [77]

73

78. *Tapster.* In other versions FitzGerald changes this to *Master* and *Savage.*

79. *Gone dry.* Omar's original has the clay beg to be made only into a bowl, suitable for drinking. Note how Fitz-Gerald's version prepares for the following quatrain.

80. *Crescent.* The new moon begins a new month, thus ending the period of fasting. It is anticipated with anxiety and hailed with rejoicing.

81. *Porter's Shoulder-knot a-creaking.* With the end of the Ramadan, the porter is coming to fill the empty pots with wine.

LXIV

Said one—"Folks of a surly Tapster [78] tell,
And daub his Visage with the Smoke of Hell;
  They talk of some strict Testing of us—Pish!
He's a Good Fellow, and 'twill all be well."

LXV

Then said another with a long-drawn Sigh,
"My Clay with long oblivion is gone dry: [79]
  But, fill me with the old familiar Juice,
Methinks I might recover by-and-bye!"

LXVI

So, while the Vessels one by one were speaking,
One spied the little Crescent [80] all were seeking:
  And then they jogg'd each other, "Brother!
    Brother!
Hark to the Porter's Shoulder-knot a-creaking!" [81]

* * * * *

82. *Gardenside*. In his Introduction, FitzGerald reports the following story told by one of Omar's pupils, Khwájah Nizámi of Samarcand: "I often used to hold conversations with my teacher, Omar Khayyám, in a garden; and one day he said to me, 'My tomb shall be in a spot where the north wind may scatter roses over it.' I wondered at the words he spake, but I knew that his were no idle words. Years after, when I chanced to revisit Naishápúr, I went to his final resting-place, and lo! it was just outside a garden, and trees laden with fruit stretched their boughs over the garden wall, and dropped their flowers upon his tomb, so that the stone was hidden under them." In 1884 William Simpson found that this tomb was the only remaining memorial of Omar. He took some rose hips from bushes growing before it and sent them to Kew Gardens, London. In 1893 a scion was taken from these transplanted bushes and planted over FitzGerald's grave in Boulge Churchyard. The plant is the *rosa centifolia.*

83. *Perfume*. In later versions, FitzGerald changed this to *Vintage*, clarifying the temptation to the True Believer, who was not supposed to indulge in alcohol.

84. Note the recurrence of the theme of repentance for the sin of drinking, first sounded in Quatrain VII and here, after the season of atonement in the Ramadan, fittingly rising to a climax.

LXVII

Ah, with the Grape my fading Life provide,
And wash my Body whence the life has died,
   And in a Windingsheet of Vineleaf wrapt,
So bury me by some sweet Gardenside.[82]

LXVIII

That ev'n my buried Ashes such a Snare
Of Perfume [83] shall fling up into the Air,
   As not a True Believer passing by
But shall be overtaken unaware.

LXIX

Indeed, the Idols I have loved so long
Have done my Credit in Men's Eye much wrong:
   Have drown'd my Honour in a shallow Cup,
And sold my Reputation for a Song.[84]

85. *Rose-in-hand.* A metaphor often used of spring, the season of roses.

86. Here FitzGerald, who has rearranged the sequence of stanzas to suit his own purposes, finally rejects the Moslem idea of repentance for indulgence in alcohol. The English poet was himself a connoisseur of liquor, but no drunkard.

87. This quatrain shows a considerable change from Omar's original, in which the Oriental poet longs for a resting-place from which he will be reborn. The Christian poet has rejected this idea for the common Western theme of regret at the passage of time and the approach of death.

LXX

Indeed, indeed, Repentance oft before
I swore—but was I sober when I swore?
   And then and then came Spring, and Rose-in-
      hand [85]
My thread-bare Penitence a-pieces tore.

LXXI

And much as Wine has play'd the Infidel,
And robb'd me of my Robe of Honour—well
   I often wonder what the Vintners buy
One half so precious as the Goods they sell.[86]

LXXII

Alas, that Spring should vanish with the Rose!
That Youth's sweet-scented Manuscript should
      close!
   The Nightingale that in the Branches sang,
Ah, whence, and whither flown again, who knows! [87]

88. This stanza has aroused some literary comment. Paul Elmer More, in "Why Is Browning Popular?," cites the passage as descriptive of Browning's attitude toward love. O. Henry, in his "The Rubáiyát of a Scotch Highball" (see note on Quatrain VII) has the husband, who has in vain tried to forswear drink, recite this stanza with his wife in a final and successful effort to give up alcohol.

89. *Moon of my Delight . . . Moon of Heav'n*. This is another instance of parallel phraseology, of which FitzGerald was so fond and which, with repetition, achieves a new dimension. Compare the uses of this device in Quatrains VII, XIX, XXII, XXIII, XXXI, and elsewhere.

90. *TAMÁM SHUD*. "The very end." Since the work has been very popular, it has had many parodies. One of the closest and most amusing is Oliver Herford's "The Rubáiyát of a Persian Kitten." Another, which exhibits very remote parallels indeed is James Whitcomb Riley's "The Rubáiyát of Doc Sifers." The latter runs on to 105 stanzas of 14-syllable lines, rimed *aabb*. However, both works end with the above closing words in Persian.

LXXIII

Ah, Love! could thou and I with Fate conspire
To grasp this sorry Scheme of Things entire,
   Would not we shatter it to bits—and then
Re-mould it nearer to the Heart's Desire! [88]

LXXIV

Ah, Moon of my Delight who know'st no wane,
The Moon of Heav'n [89] is rising once again:
   How oft hereafter rising shall she look
Through this same Garden after me—in vain!

LXXV

And when Thyself with shining Foot shall pass
Among the Guests Star-scatter'd on The Grass,
   And in Thy joyous Errand reach the Spot
Where I made one—turn down an empty Glass!

TAMÁM SHUD [90]

RUBÁIYÁT
of
OMAR KHAYYÁM

(Fifth Version)

I

WAKE! For the Sun, who scatter'd into flight
The Stars before him from the Field of Night,
  Drives Night along with them from Heav'n, and
    strikes
The Sultán's Turret with a Shaft of Light.

II

Before the phantom of False morning died,
Methought a Voice within the Tavern cried,
  "When all the Temple is prepared within,
"Why nods the drowsy Worshipper outside?"

III

And, as the Cock crew, those who stood before
The Tavern shouted—"Open then the Door!
  "You know how little while we have to stay,
"And, once departed, may return no more."

IV

Now the New Year reviving old Desires,
The thoughtful Soul to Solitude retires,
  Where the WHITE HAND OF MOSES on the Bough
Puts out, and Jesus from the Ground suspires.

V

Iram indeed is gone with all his Rose,
And Jamshyd's Sev'n-ring'd Cup where no one
    knows;
    But still a Ruby kindles in the Vine,
And many a Garden by the Water blows.

VI

And David's lips are lockt; but in divine
High-piping Pehleví, with "Wine! Wine! Wine!
    "Red Wine!"—the Nightingale cries to the Rose
That sallow cheek of hers to' incarnadine.

VII

Come, fill the Cup, and in the fire of Spring
Your Winter-garment of Repentance fling:
    The Bird of Time has but a little way
To flutter—and the Bird is on the Wing.

VIII

Whether at Naishápúr or Babylon,
Whether the Cup with sweet or bitter run,
    The Wine of Life keeps oozing drop by drop,
The Leaves of Life keep falling one by one.

IX

Each Morn a thousand Roses brings, you say;
Yes, but where leaves the Rose of Yesterday?

And this first Summer month that brings the Rose
Shall take Jamshyd and Kaikobád away.

X

Well, let it take them! What have we to do
With Kaikobád the Great, or Kaikhosrú?

Let Zál and Rustum bluster as they will,
Or Hátim call to Supper—heed not you.

XI

With me along the strip of Herbage strown
That just divides the desert from the sown,

Where name of Slave and Sultán is forgot—
And Peace to Mahmúd on his golden Throne!

XII

A Book of Verses underneath the Bough,
A Jug of Wine, a Loaf of Bread—and Thou

Beside me singing in the Wilderness—
Oh, Wilderness were Paradise enow!

XIII

Some for the Glories of This World; and some
Sigh for the Prophet's Paradise to come;
   Ah, take the Cash, and let the Credit go
Nor heed the rumble of a distant Drum!

XIV

Look to the blowing Rose about us—"Lo,
"Laughing," she says, "into the world I blow,
   "At once the silken tassel of my Purse
"Tear, and its Treasure on the Garden throw."

XV

And those who husbanded the Golden grain,
And those who flung it to the winds like Rain,
   Alike to no such aureate Earth are turn'd
As, buried once, Men want dug up again.

XVI

The Worldly Hope men set their Hearts upon
Turns Ashes—or it prospers; and anon,
   Like Snow upon the Desert's dusty Face,
Lighting a little hour or two—is gone.

XVII

Think, in this batter'd Caravanserai
Whose Portals are alternate Night and Day,
   How Sultán after Sultán with his Pomp
Abode his destined Hour, and went his way.

XVIII

They say the Lion and the Lizard keep
The courts where Jamshyd gloried and drank deep:
   And Bahrám, that great Hunter—the Wild Ass
Stamps o'er his Head, but cannot break his Sleep.

XIX

I sometimes think that never blows so red
The Rose as where some buried Cæsar bled;
   That every Hyacinth the Garden wears
Dropt in her Lap from some once lovely Head.

XX

And this reviving Herb whose tender Green
Fledges the River-Lip on which we lean—
   Ah, lean upon it lightly! for who knows
From what once lovely Lip it springs unseen!

XXI

Ah, my Belovéd, fill the Cup that clears
To-day of past Regrets and future Fears:
    To-morrow—Why, To-morrow I may be
Myself with Yesterday's Sev'n thousand Years.

XXII

For some we loved, the loveliest and the best
That from his Vintage rolling Time hath prest,
    Have drunk their Cup a Round or two before,
And one by one crept silently to rest.

XXIII

And we, that now make merry in the Room
They left, and Summer dresses in new bloom,
    Ourselves must we beneath the Couch of Earth
Descend—ourselves to make a Couch—for whom?

XXIV

Ah, make the most of what we yet may spend,
Before we too into the Dust descend;
    Dust into Dust, and under Dust to lie,
Sans Wine, sans Song, sans Singer, and—sans End!

XXV

Alike for those who for To-DAY prepare,
And those that after some To-MORROW stare,
   A Muezzín from the Tower of Darkness cries,
"Fools! your Reward is neither Here nor There."

XXVI

Why, all the Saints and Sages who discuss'd
Of the Two Worlds so wisely—they are thrust
   Like foolish Prophets forth; their Words to Scorn
Are scatter'd, and their Mouths are stopt with Dust.

XXVII

Myself when young did eagerly frequent
Doctor and Saint, and heard great argument
   About it and about: but evermore
Came out by the same door where in I went.

XXVIII

With them the seed of Wisdom did I sow,
And with mine own hand wrought to make it grow;
   And this was all the Harvest that I reap'd—
"I came like Water, and like Wind I go."

XXIX

Into this Universe, and *Why* not knowing
Nor *Whence*, like Water willy-nilly flowing;
   And out of it, as Wind along the Waste,
I know not *Whither*, willy-nilly blowing.

XXX

What, without asking, hither hurried *Whence*?
And, without asking, *Whither* hurried hence!
   Oh, many a Cup of this forbidden Wine
Must drown the memory of that insolence!

XXXI

Up from Earth's Centre through the Seventh Gate
I rose, and on the Throne of Saturn sate,
   And many a Knot unravel'd by the Road;
But not the Master-knot of Human Fate.

XXXII

There was the Door to which I found no Key;
There was the Veil through which I might not see:
   Some little talk awhile of ME and THEE
There was—and then no more of THEE and ME.

XXXIII

Earth could not answer; nor the Seas that mourn
In flowing Purple, of their Lord Forlorn;

    Nor rolling Heaven, with all his Signs reveal'd
And hidden by the sleeve of Night and Morn.

XXXIV

Then of the THEE IN ME who works behind
The Veil, I lifted up my hands to find

    A lamp amid the Darkness; and I heard,
As from Without—"THE ME WITHIN THEE BLIND!"

XXXV

Then to the Lip of this poor earthen Urn
I lean'd, the Secret of my Life to learn:

    And Lip to Lip it murmur'd—"While you live,
"Drink!—for, once dead, you never shall return."

XXXVI

I think the Vessel, that with fugitive
Articulation answer'd, once did live,

    And drink; and Ah! the passive Lip I kiss'd,
How many Kisses might it take—and give!

XXXVII

For I remember stopping by the way
To watch a Potter thumping his wet Clay:
    And with its all-obliterated Tongue
It murmur'd—"Gently, Brother, gently, pray!"

XXXVIII

And has not such a Story from of Old
Down Man's successive generations roll'd
    Of such a clod of saturated Earth
Cast by the Maker into Human mould?

XXXIX

And not a drop that from our Cups we throw
For Earth to drink of, but may steal below
    To quench the fire of Anguish in some Eye
There hidden—far beneath, and long ago.

XL

As then the Tulip for her morning sup
Of Heav'nly Vintage from the soil looks up,
    Do you devoutly do the like, till Heav'n
To Earth invert you—like an empty Cup.

XLI

Perplext no more with Human or Divine,
To-morrow's tangle to the winds resign,
   And lose your fingers in the tresses of
The Cypress-slender Minister of Wine.

XLII

And if the Wine you drink, the Lip you press,
End in what All begins and ends in—Yes;
   Think then you are To-day what Yesterday
You were—To-morrow you shall not be less.

XLIII

So when that Angel of the darker Drink
At last shall find you by the river-brink,
   And, offering his Cup, invite your Soul
Forth to your Lips to quaff—you shall not shrink.

XLIV

Why, if the Soul can fling the Dust aside,
And naked on the Air of Heaven ride,
   Were't not a Shame—were't not a Shame for him
In this clay carcass crippled to abide?

XLV

'Tis but a Tent where takes his one day's rest
A Sultán to the realm of Death addrest;

    The Sultán rises, and the dark Ferrash
Strikes, and prepares it for another Guest.

XLVI

And fear not lest Existence closing your
Account, and mine, should know the like no more;

    The Eternal Sákí from that Bowl has pour'd
Millions of Bubbles like us, and will pour.

XLVII

When You and I behind the Veil are past,
Oh, but the long, long while the World shall last,

    Which of our Coming and Departure heeds
As the Sea's self should heed a pebble-cast.

XLVIII

A Moment's Halt—a momentary taste
Of BEING from the Well amid the Waste—

    And Lo!—the phantom Caravan has reach'd
The NOTHING it set out from—Oh, make haste!

XLIX

Would you that spangle of Existence spend
About THE SECRET—quick about it, Friend!
   A Hair perhaps divides the False from True—
And upon what, prithee, may life depend?

L

A Hair perhaps divides the False and True;
Yes; and a single Alif were the clue—
   Could you but find it—to the Treasure-house,
And peradventure to THE MASTER too;

LI

Whose secret Presence through Creation's veins
Running Quicksilver-like eludes your pains;
   Taking all shapes from Máh to Máhi and
They change and perish all—but He remains;

LII

A moment guess'd—then back behind the Fold
Immerst of Darkness round the Drama roll'd
   Which, for the Pastime of Eternity,
He doth Himself contrive, enact, behold.

LIII

But if in vain, down on the stubborn floor
Of Earth, and up to Heav'n's unopening Door,
   You gaze To-DAY, while You are You—how then
To-MORROW, when You shall be You no more?

LIV

Waste not your Hour, nor in the vain pursuit
Of This and That endeavour and dispute;
   Better be jocund with the fruitful Grape
Than sadden after none, or Bitter, Fruit.

LV

You know, my friends, with what a brave Carouse
I made a Second Marriage in my house;
   Divorced old barren Reason from my Bed,
And took the Daughter of the Vine to Spouse.

LVI

For "Is" and "Is-not" though with Rule and Line
And "UP-AND-DOWN" by Logic I define,
   Of all that one should care to fathom, I
Was never deep in anything but—Wine.

LVII

Ah, by my Computations, People say,
Reduce the Year to better reckoning?—Nay,
   'Twas only striking from the Calendar
Unborn To-morrow and dead Yesterday.

LVIII

And lately, by the Tavern Door agape,
Came shining through the Dusk an Angel Shape
   Bearing a Vessel on his Shoulder; and
He bid me taste of it; and 'twas—the Grape!

LIX

The Grape that can with Logic absolute
The Two-and-Seventy jarring Sects confute:
   The sovereign Alchemist that in a trice
Life's leaden metal into Gold transmute;

LX

The mighty Mahmúd, Allah-breathing Lord,
That all the misbelieving and black Horde
   Of Fears and Sorrows that infest the Soul
Scatters before him with his whirlwind Sword.

LXI

Why, be this Juice the growth of God, who dare
Blaspheme the twisted tendril as a Snare?
    A Blessing, we should use it, should we not?
And if a Curse—why, then, Who set it there?

LXII

I must abjure the Balm of Life, I must,
Scared by some After-reckoning ta'en on trust,
    Or lured with Hope of some Diviner Drink,
To fill the Cup—when crumbled into Dust!

LXIII

Of threats of Hell and Hopes of Paradise!
One thing at least is certain—*This* Life flies;
    One thing is certain and the rest is Lies;
The Flower that once has blown for ever dies.

LXIV

Strange, is it not? that of the myriads who
Before us pass'd the door of Darkness through,
    Not one returns to tell us of the Road,
Which to discover we must travel too.

LXV

The Revelations of Devout and Learn'd
Who rose before us, and as Prophets burn'd,
　　Are all but Stories, which, awoke from Sleep
They told their comrades, and to Sleep return'd.

LXVI

I sent my Soul through the Invisible,
Some letter of that After-life to spell:
　　And by and by my Soul return'd to me,
And answer'd "I Myself am Heav'n and Hell:"

LXVII

Heav'n but the Vision of fulfill'd Desire,
And Hell the Shadow from a Soul on fire,
　　Cast on the Darkness into which Ourselves,
So late emerged from, shall so soon expire.

LXVIII

We are no other than a moving row
Of Magic Shadow-shapes that come and go
　　Round with the Sun-illumined Lantern held
In Midnight by the Master of the Show;

LXIX

But helpless Pieces of the Game He plays.
Upon this Chequer-board of Nights and Days;
    Hither and thither moves, and checks, and slays
And one by one back in the Closet lays.

LXX

The Ball no question makes of Ayes and Noes,
But Here or There as strikes the Player goes;
    And He that toss'd you down into the Field,
He knows about it all—HE knows—HE knows!

LXXI

The Moving Finger writes; and, having writ,
Moves on: nor all your Piety nor Wit
    Shall lure it back to cancel half a Line,
Nor all your Tears wash out a Word of it.

LXXII

And that inverted Bowl they call the Sky,
Whereunder crawling coop'd we live and die,
    Lift not your hands to *It* for help—for It
As impotently moves as you or I.

LXXIII

With Earth's first Clay They did the Last Man
knead,
And there of the Last Harvest sow'd the Seed:
And the first Morning of Creation wrote
What the Last Dawn of Reckoning shall read.

LXXIV

YESTERDAY *This* Day's Madness did prepare;
TO-MORROW's Silence, Triumph, or Despair:
Drink! for you not know whence you came,
nor why:
Drink! for you know not why you go nor where.

LXXV

I tell you this—When, started from the Goal,
Over the flaming shoulders of the Foal
Of Heav'n Parwín and Mushtarí they flung,
In my predestined Plot of Dust and Soul.

LXXVI

The Vine had struck a fiber: which about
It clings my Being—let the Dervish flout;
Of my Base metal may be filed a Key
That shall unlock the Door he howls without.

LXXVII

And this I know: whether the one True Light
Kindle to Love, or Wrath-consume me quite,
  One Flash of It within the Tavern caught
Better than in the Temple lost outright.

LXXVIII

What! out of senseless Nothing to provoke
A conscious Something to resent the yoke
  Of unpermitted Pleasure, under pain
Of Everlasting Penalties, if broke!

LXXIX

What! from his helpless Creature be repaid
Pure Gold for what he lent him dross-allay'd—
  Sue for a Debt he never did contract,
And cannot answer—Oh the sorry trade!

LXXX

Oh Thou, who didst with pitfall and with gin
Beset the Road I was to wander in,
  Thou wilt not with Predestined Evil round
Enmesh, and then impute my Fall to Sin!

LXXXI

Oh Thou, who Man of baser Earth didst make,
And ev'n with Paradise devise the Snake:
   For all the Sin wherewith the Face of Man
Is blacken'd—Man's forgiveness give—and take!

* * * * *

LXXXII

As under cover of departing Day
Slunk hunger-stricken Ramazán away,
   Once more within the Potter's house alone
I stood, surrounded by the Shapes of Clay.

LXXXIII

Shapes of all Sorts and Sizes, great and small,
That stood along the floor and by the wall;
   And some loquacious Vessels were; and some
Listen'd perhaps, but never talk'd at all.

LXXXIV

Said one among them—"Surely not in vain
"My substance of the common Earth was ta'en
   "And to this Figure moulded, to be broke,
"Or trampled back to shapeless Earth again."

LXXXV

Then said a Second—"Ne'er a peevish Boy
"Would break the Bowl from which he drank in
    joy;
  "And he that with his hand the Vessel made
"Will surely not in after Wrath destroy."

LXXXVI

After a momentary silence spake
Some Vessel of a more ungainly make;
  "They sneer at me for leaning all awry:
"What! did the Hand then of the Potter shake?"

LXXXVII

Whereat some one of the loquacious Lot—
I think a Súfi pipkin—waxing hot—
  "All this of Pot and Potter—Tell me, then,
"Who is the Potter, pray, and who the Pot?"

LXXXVIII

"Why," said another, "Some there are who tell
"Of one who threatens he will toss to Hell
  "The luckless Pots he marr'd in making—Pish!
"He's a Good Fellow, and 'twill all be well."

LXXXIX

"Well," murmured one, "Let whoso make or buy,
"My Clay with long Oblivion is gone dry:
    "But fill me with the old familiar Juice,
"Methinks I might recover by and by."

XC

So while the Vessels one by one were speaking,
The little Moon look'd in that all were seeking:
    And then they jogg'd each other, "Brother!
        "Brother!
"Now for the Porter's shoulder-knot a-creaking!"

*   *   *   *   *

XCI

Ah, with the Grape my fading life provide,
And wash the Body whence the Life has died,
    And lay me, shrouded in the living Leaf,
By some not unfrequented Garden-side.

XCII

That ev'n my buried Ashes such a snare
Of Vintage shall fling up into the Air
    As not a True-believer passing by
But shall be overtaken unaware.

XCIII

Indeed the Idols I have loved so long
Have done my credit in this World much wrong:
 Have drown'd my Glory in a shallow Cup,
And sold my Reputation for a Song.

XCIV

Indeed, indeed, Repentance oft before
I swore—but was I sober when I swore?
 And then and then came Spring, and
    Rose-in-hand
My thread-bare Penitence apieces tore.

XCV

And much as Wine has play'd the Infidel,
And robb'd me of my Robe of Honour—Well,
 I wonder often what the Vintners buy
One half so precious as the stuff they sell.

XCVI

Yet Ah, that Spring should vanish with the Rose!
That Youth's sweet-scented manuscript should
    close!
 The Nightingale that in the branches sang,
Ah whence, and whither flown again, who knows!

XCVII

Would but the Desert of the Fountain yield
One glimpse—if dimly, yet indeed, reveal'd,
　To which the fainting Traveller might spring,
As springs the trampled herbage of the field!

XCVIII

Would but some wingéd Angel ere too late
Arrest the yet unfolded Roll of Fate,
　And make the stern Recorder otherwise
Enregister, or quite obliterate!

XCIX

Ah Love! could you and I with Him conspire
To grasp this sorry Scheme of Things entire,
　Would not we shatter it to bits—and then
Re-mould it nearer to the Heart's Desire!

* * * * *

C

Yon rising Moon that looks for us again—
How oft hereafter will she wax and wane;
　How oft hereafter rising look for us
Through this same Garden—and for *one* in vain!

CI

And when like her, oh Sákí, you shall pass
Among the Guests Star-scatter'd on the Grass,
    And in your joyous errand reach the spot
Where I made One—turn down an empty Glass!

TAMÁM.

QUESTIONS FOR DISCUSSION

The following questions are designed to stimulate
thought and to develop appreciation of both the
ideas and poetic qualities of the poem. In some
cases, several different answers are equally accept-
able. The numbers of the stanzas refer to the First
Version.

I

Who is the *Hunter of the East*?

Why is it the *Turret* that he has caught *in a Noose
of Light*?

How does this stanza set the mood for the poem's
main theme, expressed in the next stanza?

II

This stanza proclaims the poem's theme. What is it?

What important symbols employed throughout the
poem are introduced here? What does each represent?

III

When do the visitors come to the *Tavern*? Why is
the time significant?

IV

A new idea is introduced here, of great importance
to the rest of the poem. What is it?
It is spring, but what does the *thoughtful Soul* do?
Why? Is the idea appropriate to the season according to Moslem belief?

V

What do *Irám* and the *Cup* represent?
How do the *Vine* and *Garden* contrast with these
symbols?

VI

How and why might the *yellow Cheek* of the Rose
become incarnadined?

VII

Why is *Repentance* a *Winter Garment*, and *Spring*
a *Fire*?
What is the philosophy expressed in this stanza?
Is this in accord with Jewish, Christian, or Moslem belief?

VIII

What do *Blossoms*, *Jamshyd*, and *Kaikobád* have
in common?

IX

Each of the Persian heroes in this stanza has a special significance. What is it? What does the poem say about their importance?

X

What reasons might be advanced for Omar to take his beloved *along some Strip of Herbage strown / That just divides the desert from the sown?*

XI

Do you think the symbolic Súfi interpretation of *desert*, *Wilderness*, and *Paradise* is appropriate here? Why?

XII

What does the third line mean?

What is the significance of the *distant Drum?*

We now begin the theme of the impermanence of what men commonly value. What is the first?

In the final revision, FitzGerald substituted the word *rumble* for *music*. Which do you prefer? Why?

XIII

What is shown to be transient in this quatrain?

XIV

What meaning or meanings are intended by *lighting* in the fourth line?

What does the poet say will not last?

XV

Note how the theme of the color gold is employed. Where is it first cited? What other references are made to it? Why do you think the poet has chosen this symbol? What does it represent?

Explain the irony in the last two lines of this quatrain.

XVI

Why is the *Caravanserai batter'd*? What does it symbolize?

XVII

Explain the significance of the *Lion,* the *Lizard,* and the *Wild Ass.*

XVIII

How does the poet account for the redness of the *Rose* and the loveliness of the *Hyacinth*?

XIX

What is the pun in this stanza? Is it appropriate and effective? What are your standards for judgment?

XX

Discuss the value of this solution of *past Regrets and future Fears.*

XXI

Explain the symbolism of the first two lines.

XXII

Is this a sensible or selfish philosophy?

XXIII

What is the origin of the third line?

Compare the philosophy expressed here with that of the Biblical passages which inspired the imagery.

XXIV

Because, from the height of the minaret, the muezzin can see into the private chambers of the surrounding houses, the responsibility is often given to a blind man. What pertinence, if any, does this have to the poet's idea?

What Arabic words does the muezzin actually cry? What do they mean? How do you think Mohammedans would regard this stanza?

The reference to the muezzin is not in Omar's original. What would be the Christian equivalent? What effect do you think Christian belief had upon this "translation"?

XXV

What are the *Two Worlds*?

Why does the poet call the *Saints and Sages foolish Prophets*?

XXVI

Why are you encouraged to *leave the wise / To talk*?

XXVII

What is the *same Door* by which the poet both entered and departed?

XXVIII

What is the *Seed of Wisdom*? With whom did he sow it? What did he learn as a result?

XXIX

In your own words, what three questions are asked? What are the author's answers? What are yours?

XXX

What is the *Impertinence*?

XXXI

What does the poet's ascent from the center of the Earth to Saturn represent? Is this a good metaphor? Why?

XXXII

What are the *Door* and the *Veil*?
Why does the *Talk . . . of ME and THEE* cease?
Why is there a colon after *see*?

XXXIII

What answer does Heaven give to the riddle? Is it satisfactory?

XXXIV

What answer does the poet give?
What is the *secret Well of Life*?

XXXV

What *Lip* is the poet kissing?
Why does he speak of *fugitive / Articulation*?

XXXVI

What is the significance of the Clay's remark to the Potter? Why does he call the Potter *Brother*?

XXXVII

The poet uses contrast very effectively here: analyze
it.

What does the *Caravan* represent?

Give an example of irony in this quatrain.

XXXVIII

To whose comments is the poet objecting?

XXXIX

Is this stanza more typical of Omar or FitzGerald?
Why? See the lives of each in the Introduction.

What is the effect of repeating *How long*?

XL

Why does the poet divorce *Reason*?

XLI

Whose occupation is reflected in the first two lines?
Explain.

Do you think the statement in the last two lines
accurately reflects the life of Omar or FitzGerald?

XLII

In later versions FitzGerald substituted *shining* for
stealing. Which do you prefer? Why?

Why do you think the poet retained the initial
hissing sound? What is this figure of speech
called?

XLIII

How can the Grape confute the quarreling sects
and change lead into gold?

XLIV

Compare the religious views implied in this and
the following quatrain.

XLV

What is *making Game* of humanity?
Why would this stanza antagonize both orthodox
Mohammedans and Súfis? What would be the
attitude of Christians toward it?

XLVI

In what ways is this an effective or ineffective
comparison?

XLVII

In the final analysis, what does the poet say Man
can lose? Why?
What is your opinion of this philosophy?

XLVIII

What is the *darker Draught*?
What attitude does the poet recommend when that
drink is offered?
Is this harmonious with his general philosophy of
life?

XLIX

Does the poet believe in Fate or Providence? What is the difference between the two terms?

L

What game is referred to? Compare the meaning of this metaphor with that of Quatrain XLVI.

LI

Compare the intention of the Biblical passage with this.

LII

Why is the image of the Bowl especially appropriate?

LIII

If this philosophy were universally followed, how would it affect our society? How would it affect your own life?

LIV

What does the poet suggest had a powerful influence on his life?

LV

What is the poet's attitude toward the Súfis? What are the *Base Metal* and the *Door*?

LVI

What attitudes toward religion are suggested here?

LVII

What religious paradox is the poet attacking?

LVIII

Why do some critics consider this stanza blasphemous?

LIX

In what ways is it appropriate to compare men to clay pots?

LX

What is the meaning of the question in the final line?

What answers would be given by the believers in predestination? in the dominant significance of environment? in the significance of heredity?

LXI

What religious philosophy is expressed here?

LXII

What optimistic argument does the poet advance in this quatrain?

121

LXIII

What is the enigma in this stanza? How would you answer it?

LXIV

Who is the *Tapster*? Is this a good metaphor in view of the philosophy expressed by this pot?

FitzGerald substituted *Master* and *Savage* for *Tapster* in other versions. Which is the best? Why?

LXV

What will cure this pot of his melancholy?

LXVI

Summarize the problems presented by the pots. With what religious philosophies do they agree and conflict?

Why have the pots been dry? Why is the wine arriving *now*?

LXVII

What seems to be the author's thoughts on the Afterlife? Is this harmonious with his general philosophy? Why? On this basis, do you judge that his ideas, as expressed in this poem, are sentimental or serious? (Look up the definition of the word *sentimental* in a good dictionary before answering.)

LXVIII

Why will his ashes fling *a Snare of Perfume* into
  the air?

Why is it a *True Believer* who is to be *overtaken
  unaware*? What would his reaction be? Why do
  you think FitzGerald suggested that he might be
  so *overtaken*?

LXIX

What are the *Idols*?

What has *done my Credit in Men's Eye much
  wrong*?

LXX

This stanza is based upon the same original as
  VII. Compare them. Which do you prefer? Why?
What destroyed the poet's resolution?

LXXI

How has *Wine . . . play'd the Infidel*?
What is the poet's final evaluation of his loss?

LXXII

What time of the day, the year, and life is this?
What are the clues?

LXXIII

What changes do you think the poet would make?
Is it likely that, if the poet *grasped this sorry
Scheme of Things entire,* his remolding of the
world would differ from his present anticipa-
tion? Why?

LXXIV

Why is the parallelism of the metaphor in the first
two lines so effective?
How does the setting enhance the mood?

LXXV

What is the significance of *turn down an empty
Glass?*
Tamám means *the end;* why has the poet added
shud?

PROBLEMS FOR
INDIVIDUAL RESEARCH

1. Omar Khayyám, mathematician and astronomer.
2. The religious beliefs and affiliations of Omar Khayyám.
3. Omar Khayyám and Edward FitzGerald: a comparison of their philosophies as revealed in the *Rubáiyát* and the translations.
4. The status and significance of Omar Khayyám in Persian literature.
5. How "original" is FitzGerald's translation? (Begin with Arthur J. Arberry's *Omar Khayyám: A New Version.*)
6. Edward FitzGerald as a letter-writer.
7. Edward FitzGerald as a critic.
8. Edward FitzGerald as a biographer.
9. FitzGerald's translations from the Greek.
10. FitzGerald's translations from the Spanish.
11. FitzGerald's translations from the Persian.
12. A comparison of the philosophies expressed in FitzGerald's translations of the *Rubáiyát* and *Salámán and Absál.*
13. A comparison of the versions of FitzGerald's translation of the *Rubáiyát.*

14. My friend, "Old Fitz." (Read FitzGerald's letters and see if you can discover what qualities won him friends. See Additional Reading.)
15. FitzGerald's philosophy of translation. (Consult his prefaces and letters.)
16. The *Rubáiyát* and the Bible.
17. Parodies of the *Rubáiyát*.
18. Sports and games in the *Rubáiyát*.
19. FitzGerald's poetic technique in the *Rubáiyát*.
20. A Súfi interpretation of the *Rubáiyát*.
21. FitzGerald and Alfred Lord Tennyson.
22. FitzGerald and Thomas Carlyle.
23. FitzGerald and William Makepeace Thackeray.
24. FitzGerald and E. B. Cowell.
25. Cambridge University in the first half of the nineteenth century.

COMPARATIVE TABLE OF STANZAS

IN THE FIVE VERSIONS

First	Second	Third, Fourth & Fifth
1	1	1
2	2	2
3	3	3
4	4	4
5	5	5
6	6	6
7	7	7
8	9	9
9	10	10
10	11	11
11	12	12
12	13	13
13	15	14
14	17	16
15	16	15
16	18	17
17	19	18
18	24	19
19	25	20

First	Second	Third, Fourth & Fifth
20	21	21
21	22	22
22	23	23
23	26	24
24	27	25
25	29	26
26	66	63
27	30	27
28	31	28
29	32	29
30	33	30
31	34	31
32	35	32
33	37	34
34	38	35
35	39	36
36	40	37
37		
38	49	48
39	56	54
40	57	55
41	58	56
42	60	58
43	61	59
44	62	60
45		
46	73	68
47	45	42
48	46	43
49	74	69
50	75	70

First	Second	Third, Fourth & Fifth
51	76	71
52	78	72
53	79	73
54	81	75
55	82	76
56	83	77
57	87	80
58	88	81
59	89	82
60	94	87
61	91	84
62	92	85
63	93	86
64	95	88
65	96	89
66	97	90
67	98	91
68	100	92
69	101	93
70	102	94
71	103	95
72	104	96
73	108	99
74	109	100
75	110	101
	8	8
	14	
	20	
	28	
	36	33
	41	38

First	Second	Third, Fourth & Fifth
	42	39
	43	40
	44	
	47	46
	48	47
	50	49
	51	50
	52	51
	53	52
	54	53
	55	41
	59	57
	63	61
	64	62
	65	
	67	64
	68	65
	69	44
	70	45
	71	66
	72	67
	77	
	80	74
	84	78
	85	79
	86	
	90	83
	99	
	105	97
	106	98
	107	

FITZGERALD'S MAJOR WORKS

"The Meadows in Spring." *Athenaeum, 193* (1831), 442.

"Memoir of Bernard Barton." Published in *Poems and Letters of Bernard Barton*. London, Hall, Virtue & Co., 1849.

Euphranor. Distributed privately, 1851. Printed, London and New York, John Lane, 1906.

Polonius: A Collection of Wise Saws and Modern Instances. London, William Pickering, 1852.

Six Dramas of Calderon, Freely Translated. London, William Pickering, 1853.

Euphranor, 2nd edition. London, John W. Parker & Son, 1855.

Salámán and Absál, an Allegory Translated From the Persian of Jámí. London, John W. Parker & Son, 1856.

Rubáiyát of Omar Khayyám. London, Bernard Quaritch, 1859.

Bird-Parliament. (Completed 1862, published posthumously.)

The Mighty Magician. Such Stuff as Dreams Are Made of. Distributed privately, 1865.

Rubáiyát, 2nd edition. London, Bernard Quaritch, 1868.

The Two Generals. Distributed privately, 1868.

Agamemnon. First privately distributed in 1869. London, Bernard Quaritch, 1876.

Salámán and Absál, 2nd edition. Distributed privately, 1871.

Rubáiyát, 3rd edition. London, Bernard Quaritch, 1872.

Rubáiyát of Omar Khayyám and *Salámán and Absál.* London, Bernard Quaritch, 1879. 4th edition of the *Rubáiyát* and 3rd of *Salámán and Absál.*

The Downfall and Death of King Oedipus. Distributed privately, Part I, 1880; Part II, 1881.

Readings in Crabbe's Tales of the Hall. First printed and distributed privately in 1879. London, Bernard Quaritch, 1883.

Letters of Edward FitzGerald to Fanny Kemble, 1871-1883. New York and London, Macmillan & Co., 1895.

Dictionary of Madame de Sévigné. London, Macmillan & Co., 1914. Edited by Mary Eleanor FitzGerald Kerrich.

Some New Letters of Edward FitzGerald to Bernard Barton. London, Williams and Norgate, 1923. Edited by F. R. Barton.

Edward FitzGerald's Letters to Bernard Quaritch. London, Bernard Quaritch, 1926. Edited by C. Quaritch Wrentmore.

A FitzGerald Friendship, Letters to W. B. Donne. New York, William Rudge, 1932. Edited by

Catharine Bodham Johnson and N. C. Hannay.
Letters of Edward FitzGerald. Southern Illinois
University Press, Carbondale, Illinois, 1960. Edited by J. M. Cohen. Centaur Classics.

ADDITIONAL READING

BIOGRAPHICAL

Omar Khayyám

Shirazi, J. K. M. *Life of Omar al-Khayyámi*. Edinburgh and London, T. N. Foulis, 1905.

Weir, T. H. *Omar Khayyám the Poet*. London, Murray, 1926.

Edward FitzGerald

Adams, Morley. *Omar's Interpreter*. London, Priory Press, 1910.

——*In the Footsteps of Borrow and FitzGerald*. London, Jarrold & Son, n.d.

Benson, A. C. *Edward FitzGerald*. London, Macmillan & Co., 1905. English Men of Letters Series.

Blyth, James. *Edward FitzGerald and "Posh."* London, John Long, 1908.

De Polnay, Peter. *Into an Old Room: A Memoir of Edward FitzGerald.* New York, Creative Age Press, 1949.

Glyde, John. *Life of Edward FitzGerald.* London, C. Arthur Pearson, 1900.

Groome, Francis Hindes. *Two Suffolk Friends.* Edinburgh and London, William Blackwood & Sons, 1895.

Richardson, Joanna. *Edward Fitzgerald.* London, Longmans, Green, c. 1960.

Terhune, Alfred McKinley. *The Life of Edward FitzGerald, Translator of the Rubáiyát of Omar Khayyám.* New Haven, Yale University Press, 1947.

Wright, Thomas. *The Life of Edward FitzGerald.* London, Grant Richards, 1904. 2 vols.

CRITICAL AND COMPARATIVE

Arberry, Arthur J. *Omar Khayyám: A New Version Based Upon Recent Discoveries.* New Haven, Yale University Press. 1932.

—— *The Romance of the Rubáiyát, Edward Fitz-Gerald's First Edition.* London, G. Allen & Unwin, 1959.

Arnot, Robert. *The Sufistic Quatrains of Omar Khayyám in Definitive Form Including the Translations of Edward FitzGerald (101 Quatrains) with Edward Heron-Allen's Analysis, E. H. Whinfield (500 Quatrains), J. B. Nicolas (464 Quatrains).* Universal Classics Library, New York and London, M. Walter Dunne, 1903.

Dole, Nathan Haskell. *Rubá'iyát of Omar Khayyám: English, French, German, and Danish Translations Comparatively Arranged in Accordance with the Text of Edward FitzGerald's Version.* Boston, L. C. Page, 1912.

Genung, John Franklin. *Ecclesiastes and Omar Khayyám*. New York, T. Y. Crowell & Co., c. 1901.

Heron-Allen, Edward. *Edward FitzGerald's Rubá'iyát of Omar Khayyám With Their Original Persian Sources*. London, Bernard Quaritch, 1899.

——— *The Second Edition of Edward FitzGerald's Rubá'yyát of 'Umar Khayyám*. London, Duckworth & Co., 1908.

——— *Some Sidelights Upon Edward FitzGerald's Poem, the Rubá'iyát of Omar Khayyám*. London, H. S. Nichols, 1898.

McCarthy, Justin H. *Rubáiyát of Omar Khayyám*. London, David Nutt, 1889.

Nicolas, J. B. *Les Quatrains de Khèyam*. Paris. Imprimerie Impériale, 1867.

Payne, John. *The Quatrains of Omar Kheyyam of Nishapour*. London, Villon Society, 1898.

Poore, Martha Agusta (De Santo). *The Rubáiyát and the Wine of Cana*. New York, Pageant Press, 1953.

Tutin, J. R. A. *A Concordance to FitzGerald's Translation of the Rubáiyát of Omar Khayyám*. London, Macmillan & Co., 1900.

Whinfield, Edward Henry. *The Rubá'iyát of Omar Khayyām, Edited From a Newly Discovered MS. Dated 658 (1259-1260) in the Possession of A. Chester Beatty, by A. J. Arberry, with Comparative English Versions by Edward FitzGerald, E. H. Whinfield, and the Editor*. London, E. Walker, 1949.

137

BIBLIOGRAPHICAL

Potter, Ambrose George. *A Bibliography of the Rubáiyát of Omar Khayyám, Together With Kindred Matter in Prose and Verse Pertaining Thereto*. London, Ingpen & Grant, 1929.

Prideaux, W. F. *Notes for a Bibliography of Edward FitzGerald*. London, Frank Hollings, 1901.

See also the preceding biographical and critical sources.

PARODIES

It is in some fashion the measure of the popularity of a work of literature that it is subjected to parodies. Sometimes these are humorous, sometimes trenchant, but at their best always revealing some of the basic and most memorable qualities of the original. Some of the better parodies of the *Rubáiyát* are the following:

Bacon, Josephine Daskam, "An Omar for Ladies."
Boynton, H. W., "The Golfer's Rubáiyát."
Burgess, Gelett, *The Rubáiyát of Omar Cayenne.*
Herford, Oliver, *The Rubáiyát of a Persian Kitten.*
Masterson, Kate, "The Modern Rubáiyát."
Nafe, A., *Rubáiyát of a College Student.*
Powell, Charles, "The Old Woman who Lived in a Shoe."
Riley, James Whitcomb, *Rubáiyát of Doc Sifers.*
Seaman, Owen, "Lines Written by Request."
Thompson, Francis, "Wake! for the Ruddy Ball has taken flight."
Wells, Carolyn, "The Baby's Omar."
Wells, Carolyn, *The Rubáiyát of Bridge.*

MUSICAL SETTINGS

Because the *Rubáiyát* has such melodic and exotic appeal, it has often been set to music:

Eisenmann, Will, *Rubáiyát, die Sprüche der Weisheit von Omar Khayyám, für mittlere Stimme und Klavier.*

Foote, Arthur William, *Four Character Pieces after the Rubáiyát of Omar Khayyám, for Orchestra,* Opus 48, Boston, A. P. Schmidt, c. 1912.

Lehmann, Liza, *In a Persian Garden,* a Song Cycle, including:

"Ah, Moon of My Delight." Recorded by Webster Booth, Tenor, Gramophone B 9069.

"Wake for the Sun Has Scattered into Flight."

Portnoff, Mischa, *The Rubáiyát.*

Rogers, J. H., *Five Quatrains from the Rubáiyát of Omar Khayyám Set to Music,* Boston, Ditson, c. 1914.

Salazar, Adolpho, *Rubáiyát,* a String Quartet.

Spina, Harold, *Rubáiyát of Omar Khayyám.*

RECORDINGS

Tape: *Selections From the Rubaiyat*, University of Colorado, National Tape Repository, Bureau of Audio-Visual Instruction, Boulder, Colorado, Poetic Patterns Series, 5" reel, 1-track, 7½ ips.

Disk: *Rubaiyat* and *Sohrab and Rustum*, Caedmon 1023, 33⅓.

The **AVON** Poetry Series
now contains 5 books:

Elizabeth Barrett Browning
SONNETS FROM THE
PORTUGUESE   GS11   50¢

A. E. Housman
A SHROPSHIRE LAD   GS7   50¢

Edward FitzGerald, Translator
THE RUBAIYAT OF
OMAR KHAYYAM   GS14   50¢

Samuel Taylor Coleridge
THE RIME OF THE
ANCIENT MARINER GS15   50¢

Walt Whitman
LEAVES OF GRASS   GS16   50¢

Each book includes a biography of the poet, a directory of famous quotations from the poems, questions for discussion, and suggestions for projects, additional reading, and audio-visual aids.

AMERICA IS GROWING UP WITH AVON BOOKS

THE CAMELOT LINE LEADS THE WAY